Soul of Paris

30 EXPERIENCES

BY THOMAS JONGLEZ

JONGLEZ PUBLISHING

Travel guides

'TO BREATHE PARIS
IS TO PRESERVE
ONE'S SOUL'

VICTOR HUGO

Paris is my city. I was born here, I grew up here. I often leave, I always come back.

I spend time in its cafés, restaurants, shops, historic places (particularly the secret ones) and even its hotels.

One thing I particularly like about Paris is that you never get bored. It's a perfect city for wandering around at random, with the guarantee that you'll always – and I do mean always – make delightful new discoveries: someone at the neighbouring table in a café I'd like to chat to, a new boutique or bistro, a museum that has redesigned its displays, a new secret spot …

I've been exploring the streets of my city for over 30 years now. I've written one book about its unusual shops, another about its secret bars and restaurants, and others about its unusual nights and little-known historic places. Only the last of these (*Secret Paris*) is still in print.

As for the rest, it took me a while to decide to distill the essence of my research down to my best finds – the results of a lifetime of wandering. The choices are highly personal, of course. A few secret places slipped in; others are less so. But the common denominator is that I've always come away from them saying to myself, 'Wow, what an exceptional time I've had!' – not just good (otherwise the book would be 1,000 pages long), but truly exceptional. A sort of best of the best of the city. Because Paris abhors mediocrity. Paris deserves the exceptional.

You may not always agree and you may have other suggestions. Don't hesitate to drop me a line. I'll be delighted to continue discovering new places and to add some of them to the next edition.

Enjoy!

Thomas Jonglez
thomasjonglez@editionsjonglez.com

WHAT YOU WON'T FIND
IN THIS GUIDE

- A map of the Paris metro
- How to get to Disneyland
- The most boring Michelin-starred restaurants
- The places everyone's talking about on Instagram that will
  have changed or disappeared six months from now

WHAT YOU WILL FIND
IN THIS GUIDE

- How to stargaze at the Sorbonne
- The city's most beautiful libraries
- A bistro that hasn't changed since the 1950s
- The loveliest secret spots for kissing in Paris
- The top hôtels de charme where even Parisians sometimes
  spend the night
- Where to listen to jazz in a private club open to the public by
  reservation only
- The most romantic walk in Paris
- The most beautiful restaurant in the world?

THE SYMBOLS OF
SOUL OF PARIS

< 20 €

20 to 100 €

> 100 €

Book ahead

Kiss

Spots for
kissing in Paris

Opening times often vary,
so also check the website of the place
you're planning to visit.

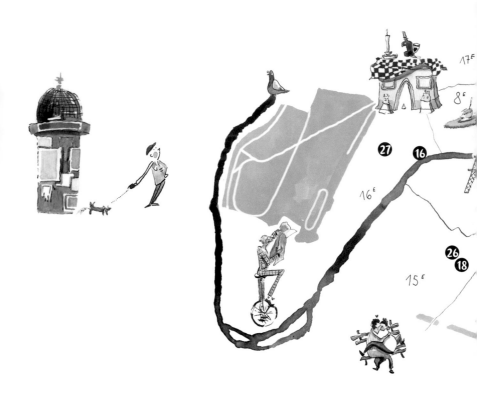

30 EXPERIENCES

17. Two fabulous suites in the heart
of Paris

18. Some of the most beautiful
lesser-known museums

19. A forgotten architectural jewel

20. Like the Place des Vosges, but
without the cars or crowds ...

21. Our kind of restaurant

22. One of the capital's greatest
architectural surprises

23. Ice cream done differently

24. The most beautiful restaurant
in the world ?

25. The go-to restaurant of many
Parisian foodies

26. The coolest thrift store in Paris

27. A cosy bar with British charm

28. Experience the sacred soul
of Paris

29. Have Montmatre all to yourself

30. A luxury hotel, like out
in the country

**#
01**

THE BEST
BAGUETTE
IN PARIS

If you aren't lucky enough to live near a top bakery or, worse still, if you don't live in Paris, you're missing out on one of life's greatest pleasures: enjoying a baguette that's so good you can eat it like cake, without butter or jam.

To experience this, we recommend choosing one of the bakeries that feature in the annual competition for the best baguette in Paris. You can't go wrong.

Listed by UNESCO as part of the Intangible Cultural Heritage of Humanity, the baguette is the French symbol par excellence. Up to six billion are produced annually in France. Every year, between 150 and 200 Parisian bakeries participate in a competition to determine the city's ten best baguettes.

Beyond the glory of carrying the day, the winner is given the great honour of becoming official supplier to the President of the Republic and the Élysée Palace for a year.

In other words, if you stop by the winning bakery, you can enjoy the same baguette as the president and his usual distinguished coterie of guests.

Participating bakers must adhere to the following requirements: they must produce 40 baguettes for the competition, each between 50 and 55 cm long, weighing between 250 and 270 grams and containing no more than 18 grams of salt per kilo of flour.

IN 2024, THE TOP TEN WINNERS WERE:

1. **BOULANGERIE UTOPIE** - 20, rue Jean-Pierre-Timbaud (11th arr.)
2. **MAISON DORÉ** - 29, rue Gay-Lussac (5th arr.)
3. **LA PARISIENNE** - 85, rue Saint-Dominique (7th arr.)
4. **BOULANGERIE ROUGÈS** - 45, avenue de Saint-Ouen (17th arr.)
5. **L'ÉCRIN GOURMAND** - 15, avenue du Docteur-Arnold-Netter (12th arr.)
6. **BOULANGERIE AA** - 63, rue du Javelot (13th arr.)
7. **BOULANGERIE PARIS AND CO** - 4, rue de la Convention (15th arr.)
8. **MAISON M** - 2, avenue de la Porte-Didot (14th arr.)
9. **AUX DÉLICES DE VAUGIRARD** - 48, rue Madame (6th arr.)
10. **DU PAIN ET VOUS** - 63, avenue Bosquet (7th arr.)

THE MOST BEAUTIFUL LIBRARIES
IN PARIS

If you've never been a student at a Parisian university, you've probably never seen inside any of the city's libraries. Which is a shame because they're among the most beautiful in the world, with architecture to rival that of any museum and the advantage that (in most cases) you can enter free of charge just by presenting your ID. So there's really nothing to stop you from sitting there for a while, just soaking up the atmosphere.

The only exception is the sublime Salle Labrouste at the Bibliothèque Nationale's Richelieu site (2nd arrondissement), which has recently been renovated and is reserved for researchers. That said, you can take a peek inside from the entrance (except on Sundays).

 BIBLIOTHÈQUE NATIONALE DE FRANCE (RICHELIEU SITE)
5, RUE VIVIENNE
75002 PARIS

Salle Labrouste (1861-1868)	**Salle Ovale** (1897-1932)	+33 1 53 79 59 59
Mon: 2pm / 7:30pm	Mon: 2pm / 7pm	Metro: Bourse
Tue–Fri: 9am / 7:30pm	Tue: 10am / 8pm	
Sat: 9am / 6:30pm	Wed–Fri: 10am / 7pm	
Sun: closed	Sat & Sun: 10am / 6pm	

BIBLIOTHÈQUE INTERUNIVERSITAIRE DE LA SORBONNE (1770)
17, RUE DE LA SORBONNE
75005 PARIS

Mon–Wed & Fri: 9am / 8pm Thu: midday / 8pm Sat: 10am / 7pm Sun: closed	+33 1 40 46 30 97 Access restricted to students, teachers, researchers and publishers	Metro: Maubert-Mutualité

BIBLIOTHÈQUE MAZARINE (1643)
23, QUAI DE CONTI
75006 PARIS

Mon–Sat: 10am / 6pm Sun: closed	+33 1 44 41 44 06 bibliotheque-mazarine.fr	Metro: Pont Neuf

BIBLIOTHÈQUE DU SÉNAT (1841)
15, RUE VAUGIRARD
75006 PARIS

Open on European Heritage Days	With a 52-metre gallery and ceiling paintings by Delacroix	Metro: Odéon

ANNEXE DE LA BIBLIOTHÈQUE DU SÉNAT (1642)
15, RUE VAUGIRARD
75006 PARIS

Open on European Heritage Days	The building housed Europe's first museum in the mid-18th century	Metro: Odéon

BIBLIOTHÈQUE HISTORIQUE DE L'ÉCOLE DE MÉDECINE (1891)
12, RUE DE L'ÉCOLE DE MÉDECINE
75006 PARIS

Mon–Sat: 9am / 8pm Sun: closed	Metro. Odéon

BIBLIOTHÈQUE DE L'HÔTEL DE VILLE (1890)
5, RUE LOBAU
75004 PARIS

Mon–Fri: 9:30am / 6pm
Sat & Sun: closed

Metro: Hôtel de Ville

BIBLIOTHÈQUE SAINTE GENEVIÈVE (1851)
10, PLACE DU PANTHÉON
75005 PARIS

Mon–Sat : 10am / 10pm Sun: closed	+33 1 44 41 97 97 bsg.univ-paris3.fr	Metro: Cluny-La Sorbonne

TWO BISTROS THAT HAVEN'T CHANGED
SINCE THE 1950S

> **Au Petit Bar:** Tucked away just 100 metres from Rue Saint-Honoré and its luxury shops, Au Petit Bar is such an unusual place in Paris that many of the locals don't even know about it.

No Wi-Fi, no credit cards, a decor that's remained unchanged for decades, a warm welcome, quality home-cooked food at very reasonable prices – and even a phone from the 1980s on the counter that actually works ...

The menu includes a few classic starters and a single dish of the day, which changes daily: salt pork with lentils, roast beef with homemade fries, and so on. Round off your meal with a dessert and voilà – you'll have a great time in a friendly atmosphere where everyone talks to everyone else.

📍 **AU PETIT BAR**
7, RUE DU MONT THABOR
75001 PARIS

| Mon–Sat: 7am / 9:30pm | +33 1 42 60 62 09 | Metro: Tuileries |

© CAELLEFUZET

> **Le Vaudésir:** Located far away from the touristy areas, Le Vaudésir is a genuinely old-fashioned bistro: period decor (early 20th century), daily specials for €8.90, home-cooked food and a no-frills atmosphere with everyone talking to each other, encouraged by the welcoming owner ... Truly our kind of place.

If the Paris of yesteryear is what you're looking for, you'll find it here, just a stone's throw from the Hôpital Sainte-Anne.

 LE VAUDÉSIR
41, RUE DAREAU
75014 PARIS

| Mon: 7:30am / 3:30pm
Tue–Fri: 7:30am / 11:30pm
Sat: 5pm / 11:30pm
Sun: closed | +33 1 43 22 03 93 | Metro: Saint-Jacques
or Mouton-Duvernet |

THE EPITOME OF
PARISIAN ELEGANCE AND CHIC

Established in 1996 just around the corner from the Louvre, Astier de Villatte is an exceptional little boutique that many consider the epitome of Parisian elegance and chic.

In a delightful 100% Parisian decor (creaky wooden floors, ancient washbasin in front of an old-fashioned staircase, etc.), you'll find the magnificent handmade ceramics the boutique is known for, as well as perfumes, candles and more.

It's expensive, of course, but sophistication comes at a price ... So why not treat yourself to a plate every now and then, as some people do, to assemble a complete, deliberately mismatched set over time?

 ASTIER DE VILLATTE
173, RUE SAINT-HONORÉ
75001 PARIS

Mon–Sat: 11am / 7pm	astierdevillatte.com	Metro: Pyramides, Tuileries ou Palais-Royal - Musée du Louvre

HAVE LUNCH
OR LISTEN TO JAZZ
IN A SWEDISH
PRIVATE CLUB

Hidden away on the second floor of a building on the Rue de Rivoli, a stone's throw from Place de la Concorde, Cercle Suédois (Swedish Circle) is a secret private club that is only open to the public on two occasions: for lunch on weekdays and for jazz evenings on Wednesdays.

In the main dining room, which overlooks the Tuileries gardens, you can savour excellent cuisine – Swedish-inspired, of course – in a calm, chic and welcoming atmosphere that even the Swedish ambassador sometimes stops by to enjoy.

 CERCLE SUÉDOIS
242, RUE DE RIVOLI
STAIRCASE A – 2ND FLOOR
75001 PARIS

Mon-Fri: midday / 2:30pm	Reservations required	
Wed: 7pm / 11pm	+33 1 42 60 76 67	
(jazz evening)	restaurant@cercle-suedois.com	Metro: Concorde

On Wednesday evenings, you can dine while taking in the jazz band (reservations required) but we prefer lingering at the bar, with its delightfully quirky retro atmosphere, sipping a cocktail or a glass of wine.

Founded in 1891, Cercle Suédois is also home to a historic room (open to the public) where, on 27 November 1895, Alfred Nobel, the inventor of dynamite, wrote his explosive will establishing the famous prize that bears his name.

 # 06

A MAGICAL STROLL
AT THE END OF THE DAY
THROUGH THE HEART
OF PARIS

There's no more perfect way to experience the magic of Paris than by going for a relaxing stroll through the centre of the city at the end of the day.

Start in the glorious gardens of the Palais-Royal, surrounded by arcades lined with pretty boutiques – the epitome of Parisian chic.

Grab a free chair and sit by the central fountain or in one of the small, enclosed gardens. Enjoy the moment, watching the comings and goings of Parisians and tourists who are all aware of being in some of the most beautiful surroundings in the world.

Leaving the gardens to the south, you'll find yourself on Place Colette. Turn left to take Passage Richelieu, which runs across the Louvre (make sure to look at the museum's pretty courtyards, visible through a large bay window) and leads to the Pyramid. The outdoor gallery of the beautiful Café Marly under the arcades is the perfect place to enjoy a drink with a view.

Continue left towards the magnificent Cour Carrée (Square Courtyard), which looks spectacular when lit up at night. Sit for a moment on the edge of the central fountain to soak up

© BENH SONG

the magic of the place before heading out to cross the Pont des Arts pedestrian bridge.

On the other side of the Seine, you have two options: either take Rue Bonaparte to Saint-Germain-des-Prés and the famous Café de Flore or the no-less famous Les Deux Magots (which is actually nicer for breakfast before 10am, without the crowds) or continue along the Seine to your left and head towards the tip of the Île de la Cité and the pedestrian quays, where you can sit and dream at the water's edge.

CINEMA,
JUST LIKE
IN THE GOOD OLD DAYS

Tired of microscopic cinemas? Feeling nostalgic for the era of the silver screen when cinemas had a capacity of 2,000 to 3,000 seats – or more – and a trip to the cinema still meant going to a show?

Then head over to the Grand Rex, one of the few cinemas in the world that survive from this golden age. Since Paris is lucky enough to be home to it, you should definitely not miss out!

Opened in 1931 and listed in 1981, the large Screen 1 (avoid the other screens, obviously) has a capacity of 2,700. In 1960, it had more visitors than the Louvre.

In addition to the main screen and its 'Mediterranean/ antique' city decor, with coloured walls that echo the Art Deco ambience of villas on the Côte d'Azur, make sure to check out the magnificent frescoes on the walls of the staircases and along the corridors leading to the main screen, which most cinema-goers overlook.

 LE GRAND REX
1, BOULEVARD POISSONNIÈRE
75002 PARIS

legrandrex.com | Metro: Bonne-Nouvelle

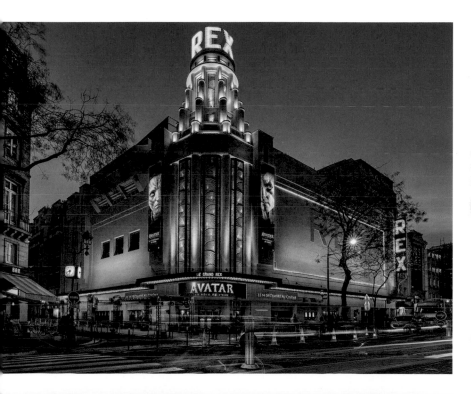

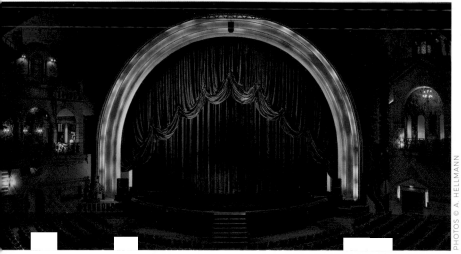

TWO PERFECT
CHIC BISTROS

Don't get them confused if you're meeting a friend: Chez Georges (2nd arrondissement) and Le Bon Georges (9th arrondissement) both have the good taste to serve classic French cuisine of the highest quality (both use the very best meat) in a pretty, very Parisian setting. Some people may consider them a bit expensive, but quality comes at a price.

CHEZ GEORGES
1, RUE DU MAIL
75002 PARIS

Mon-Fri: lunch and dinner Sat & Sun: closed	+33 1 42 60 07 11	Metro: Bourse

> **Chez Georges:** Giving trends a wide berth, Chez Georges nonetheless occasionally attracts a few stars, lured here by (among other things) the delicious pavé du mail (pan-fried steak with a mustard cream sauce), the historic decor and hand-written menus and the huge painting by J.C. Mathon from 1961 at the entrance. You might find yourself shoulder to shoulder with your neighbours, but that means you can chat with them. In summer, the outside seating area spills deliciously onto the Place des Petits-Pères.

> **Le Bon Georges:** Surprisingly little known to many Parisians, Le Bon Georges is another quality bistro, with a friendly atmosphere and a fantastic wine list. Some people think it's one of the very best bistros in Paris.

© LE PHOTOGRAPHE DU DIMANCHE - GUILLAUME SAVARY

LE BON GEORGES
45, RUE SAINT-GEORGES
75009 PARIS

| Daily: lunch and dinner | +33 1 48 78 40 30
lebongeorges.paris | Metro: Saint-Georges |

© LE PHOTOGRAPHE DU DIMANCHE · GUILLAUME SAVARY

A HOTEL WITH THE VIBE OF A FAMILY-RUN **GUESTHOUSE FROM THE LAST CENTURY**

Located in the heart of the Latin Quarter, the Hôtel des Grandes Écoles is a little gem that looks a lot like a family-run guesthouse from the last century.

Standing outside the high doors facing the street, you'd never guess what's hidden behind them: a cobbled alleyway lined with charming one-storey houses, all in a lush green setting that's rare in Paris. Having breakfast on the terrace under the trees in fine weather is a pure delight.

There's only one slight drawback: some of the beautiful rooms, with their old-fashioned decor, are quite small. But you can hardly expect a three-star hotel to be a palace ...

 HÔTEL DES GRANDES ÉCOLES
75, RUE DU CARDINAL LEMOINE
75005 PARIS

| +33 1 43 26 79 23 | hoteldesgrandesecoles.com | Metro: Cardinal Lemoine |

STARGAZING
AT THE SORBONNE

It's one of central Paris's best-kept secrets. Twice a week, on Monday and Friday after sunset, five lucky individuals are granted access to the Sorbonne Observatory for an extraordinary evening: observing the moon and the heavens from the heart of Paris, with a guide from the Société Astronomique de France (French Astronomical Society).

Spend an unforgettable evening gazing up at the stars in a timeless atmosphere that could be straight out of *Tintin and the Shooting Star*.

Tickets to this magical experience are hard to come by, so don't miss your chance to book a spot: at the end of each month, you can make reservations for the following month.

OBSERVATOIRE DE LA SORBONNE
17, RUE DE LA SORBONNE
75005 PARIS

| Mon & Fri: depending on when the sun sets | boutique.saf-astronomie.fr/produit/ visite-de-lobservatoire-de-la-sorbonne | Metro: Cluny-La Sorbonne |

FRENCH
CHIC

Does the huge number of so-called hôtels de charme in the capital leave your head spinning? Are you looking for a perfectly located (in other words, not near the Champs-Élysées), typically Parisian hotel that epitomises French chic?

Here are two fabulous options.

> **Hôtel de l'Abbaye** (Saint-Germain-des-Prés), for its timeless classic-chic style, a fireplace where you can sit and enjoy a drink in winter (reserve your spot at the reception), a small garden and the invisible presence of former guests, such as Marcello Mastroianni.

📍 **HÔTEL DE L'ABBAYE**
10, RUE CASSETTE
75006 PARIS

+33 1 45 44 38 11 | hotelabbayeparis.com
reception@hotelabbayeparis.com | Metro: Saint-Sulpice

© FRANCK FRIGNET

> **Le Pavillon de la Reine** (Marais), which has the great advantage of overlooking the gorgeous Place des Vosges. In winter, a fire crackles in the fireplace in the entrance lounge from breakfast through dinner (open to non-guests). In summer, a very pleasant terrace awaits you in the inner courtyard, not to mention a lovely little underground spa with a jacuzzi and a hammam.

 **LE PAVILLON DE LA REINE
28, PLACE DES VOSGES
75003 PARIS**

+33 1 40 29 19 19	pavillon-de-la-reine.com contact@pdlr.fr	Metro: Chemin Vert

© DAVID GRIMBERT

© JEROME GALLAND

AUGUSTIN,
CULINARY ARTIST

You can count Parisian restaurants like this on the fingers of one hand: more than simply lunch or dinner, Augustin Marchand d'Vins offers a true experience in every sense of the word.

A former resident of the Villa Medici, where he was employed as a culinary artist, Augustin has retained his appreciation of quality and good presentation from his time in Rome. On four evenings a week (Thursday to Sunday), guests are served one dish, and one dish only, which is a genuine artistic creation. Beware: there won't be enough for everyone!

In this intimate setting, the high-quality cuisine enhanced by a fanciful je ne sais quoi just adds to the delight.

Not to be missed!

 AUGUSTIN MARCHAND D'VINS
26, RUE DES GRANDS AUGUSTINS
75006 PARIS

Thu-Sun: 5pm / 10pm	+33 9 81 21 76 21 augustin75006@gmail.com augustinmarchand.com	Metro: Odéon

ALL THE MAGIC
OF THE CAPITAL

Most Parisians – let alone tourists – don't often think of going into the École des beaux-arts. Which is a shame because, thanks to the frequent exhibitions held there, it's often possible to get in and linger for a while in the school's uniquely romantic atmosphere.

Between the many copies of famous artworks to be seen here and there, work by students from all eras (recent and not so recent), the eclectic architecture of the various buildings, the magnificent Palais des Études and the remarkable Florentine-style cloister in the Cour des Mûriers (Mulberry Courtyard), you'll feel you can almost touch the magic of the capital.

Don't miss the chapel of the former monastery of the Petits Augustins friars when it's open.

 ÉCOLE DES BEAUX-ARTS DE PARIS
14, RUE BONAPARTE
75006 PARIS

Open for exhibitions and organised events, such as European Heritage Days (September), information days (early February) and open studios days (last weekend in June)	+33 1 47 03 50 74 beauxartsparis.fr	Metro: Saint-Germain-des-Prés

A TRUE
CABINET OF CURIOSITIES

Some people come here as if they were visiting a natural history museum or a cabinet of curiosities, and that's fine.

Others come to treat themselves: a stuffed lion or zebra for the hallway, a meteorite or a chunk of Mars for the coffee table or, for those with more limited budgets, a magnificent butterfly with azure wings ...

Unless of course you opt for a polar bear, a crocodile, an iridescent beetle, a spider or (more wisely) a herbarium press or one of the famous educational posters that made the company such a success in the late 19th century.

Founded in 1831 in a magnificent town house built between 1697 and 1699, the venerable Deyrolle is still the go-to place in France for taxidermy and entomology.

 **DEYROLLE**
46, RUE DU BAC
75007 PARIS

| Mon–Sat: 10am / 7pm | +33 1 42 22 30 07 deyrolle.com | Metro: Rue du Bac |

CRUISING
ON THE SEINE
IN STYLE

Have you always thought that cruising on the Seine could be great, but that the Bateaux Mouches, with their hordes of tourists and pre-recorded announcements blaring over loudspeakers, just weren't for you?

We get it.

Since 2021, Le Bateau Français has had the good idea of offering a 90-minute 'chic' cruise with champagne and everything you need for a festive or romantic experience – your choice. All on a magnificent, luxurious retro 30s-style boat, made in France in La Rochelle.

LE BATEAU FRANÇAIS

Closed from mid-January to mid-March From 1 to 8 passengers	lebateaufrancais.com contact@lebateaufrancais.com	Boarding at: Louvre, Musée d'Orsay, Port des Champs-Élysées or Saint-Germain-des-Prés

VISITING THE CITY'S MAJOR MUSEUMS AT NIGHT

Paris, like many other cities in the world, suffers from over-tourism. The sometimes disrespectful crowds that descend on museums like the Louvre and the Musée d'Orsay inevitably ruin the experience a little.

The best way to see the world's most beautiful museums and some of the city's other gems is to visit them at night.

The Louvre on Fridays, the Musée d'Orsay on Thursdays: you'll find all the magic of their collections – and the night adds an extra layer of mystery, perfect for a solitary visit or for luring in a passing tourist. Not to mention that once the sun goes down, strange things sometimes happen in museums, like the man we saw stepping over the security cordons and surreptitiously throwing himself on a Babylonian tombstone to absorb its energy – an instant stolen from eternity.

MUSÉE D'ORSAY – Thursday until 9:45pm
MUSÉE DU LOUVRE – Friday until 9:45pm
MUSÉE DES ARTS ET MÉTIERS – Friday until 9pm
MUSÉE D'ART MODERNE DE PARIS – Thursday until 9:30pm for temporary exhibitions
BOURSE DU COMMERCE – Friday until 9pm
MUSÉE DES ARTS DÉCORATIFS – Thursday until 9pm

TWO FABULOUS SUITES
IN THE HEART OF PARIS

Are you tired of standardised luxury hotel rooms that are the same whether you're in Paris, Tokyo or New York? Do you like spending time in exceptional places where taste and refinement are evident in every detail? Do you have a sizeable budget but prefer to spend your money wisely?

Then look no further than the Cinabre Suites.

Located above the boutique of the same name, which specialises in men's accessories (dressing gowns, slippers, ties, etc.), these two suites, each measuring roughly 80 square metres, are a true celebration of Parisian art de vivre and French artisanship.

LES SUITES CINABRE
14, CITÉ BERGÈRE
75009 PARIS

+33 6 76 05 07 09 | suitescinabre.com | Metro: Grands Boulevards

What the two have in common is that they are the only hotel bedrooms in France where you can sleep on a famous Hästens mattress, considered by many to be the best in the world.

Luxurious bedding, rare spirits in the bar, vinyl turntables in the rooms, top-quality cosmetics … You'll feel like you're in a cocoon.

While the building and the street itself may not be the stuff of dreams, this very central district is teeming with excellent bars and restaurants, just a few minutes' walk away.

SOME OF THE
MOST BEAUTIFUL
LESSER-KNOWN MUSEUMS

Paris may have some of the finest museums in the world, but it's best to avoid the Louvre and the Musée d'Orsay during the day, when they're overrun with tourists. If you don't want to wait until nighttime (see page 84), one option is to visit the city's smaller museums that don't attract the crowds. Some are absolutely magnificent and guarantee an authentic, off-the-beaten-track experience.

Our favourites: the Musée Gustave Moreau (9th arrondissement) for its atmosphere and wonderful staircase; the Musée Nissim de Camondo (8th arrondissement) for the beauty of the town house, its 19th-century collections and its historic kitchens; the Musée Bourdelle (15th arrondissement) for the artist's magnificent studio and the sculptures scattered around the garden; and the Musée Jean-Jacques Henner (17th arrondissement).

At the Musée Nissim de Camondo, take advantage of the restaurant located in a beautiful inner courtyard next to the museum.

 MUSÉE GUSTAVE MOREAU
14, RUE CATHERINE DE LA ROCHEFOUCAULD
75009 PARIS

Mon: 10am / 12:30pm and 2:30pm / 6pm	+33 1 83 62 78 72	Metro:
Tue: closed	musee-moreau.fr	Trinité - d'Estienne d'Orves
Wed–Sun: 10am / 12:30pm and 2:30pm / 6pm		

MUSÉE NISSIM DE CAMONDO
63, RUE DE MONCEAU
75008 PARIS

| Mon & Tue: closed
Wed–Sun: 10am / 5:30pm | +33 1 53 89 06 50
madparis.fr/Musee-Nissim-de-Camondo-125 | Metro: Villiers |

© HARTL-MEYER

© HARTL-MEYER

MUSÉE NATIONAL JEAN-JACQUES HENNER
43, AVENUE DE VILLIERS
75017 PARIS

Mon: 11am / 6pm
Tue: closed
Wed–Sun: 11am / 6pm

+33 1 83 62 56 17
musee-henner.fr

Metro: Malesherbes

A FORGOTTEN
ARCHITECTURAL JEWEL

Are you desperate for some peace and quiet after being jostled by the tourist hordes in the grands magasins? Or do you simply happen to be in the Opéra district, completely unaware that there's an architectural jewel hidden just around the corner? Located a short walk away, on Boulevard Haussmann, it's one of Paris's biggest secrets, the historic headquarters of Société Générale, founded in 1912.

When the bank is open (because, yes, the main office is still in operation and continues to serve customers), saunter in and admire the spectacular circular counter (known as *le fromage*, 'the cheese') under an enormous glass dome with a steel frame (24 metres in diameter) designed by Jacques Galland.

The magnificent mosaic floors were created by Alphonse Gentil and François-Eugène Bourdet. In the basement, take a peek at the main armoured door to the vault, which is 40 cm thick and weighs 18 tonnes.

But remember to be discreet – this is, after all, first and foremost a place of work.

 HISTORICAL HEADQUARTERS OF SOCIÉTÉ GÉNÉRALE
29, BOULEVARD HAUSSMANN
75009 PARIS

Mon & Tue: 9am / 5:30pm Wed: 9am / 10am and 11am / 5:30pm Thu & Fri: 9am / 5:30pm Sun: closed	Also open on heritage days	Metro: Chaussée d'Antin - La Fayette

LIKE THE PLACE DES VOSGES,
BUT WITHOUT THE CARS OR CROWDS ...

When you need to escape the noise and bustle of the capital, there's a gorgeous and unexpected spot in the 10th arrondissement that's perfect for a quiet break.

Some people describe the magnificent inner courtyard of the old Hôpital Saint-Louis as a Place des Vosges ... without the cars or the crowds. Which gives you a pretty good idea of just how charming and beautiful it is.

Now a listed historic monument, the old hospital was built in response to the great plague epidemic of 1562, which killed more than 68,000 people in Paris.

The flowerbeds in the centre of the lawn were designed to evoke a Maltese cross. Today, one of the hospital's pavilions is home to the Order of Malta, an ancient hospitaller order.

 COURTYARD OF THE OLD HÔPITAL SAINT-LOUIS
40, RUE BICHAT ET 1, AVENUE CLAUDE VELLEFAUX
75010 PARIS

| Daily: 8am / 6pm | +33 1 42 49 49 49 | Metro: Goncourt or Jacques Bonsergent |

OUR KIND OF
RESTAURANT

We love everything about Billili: the decor (simple and tasteful), the food (excellent; one or two real dishes but mainly tapas), the atmosphere (lively and cheerful), the service (friendly), the prices (very reasonable) and also the fact that they don't take reservations. Apart from the obvious drawback of not being able to guarantee you'll get a table there in the evening (it's easier at lunchtime), this means that you can stop by for lunch or dinner on a whim, unlike at most other (good) restaurants in the capital. Long live spontaneity!

Of course, to get seated for dinner without having to wait until 10pm, you'll have to arrive on the early side (around 7:30pm) ...

For those who prefer to play it safe, Les Arlots, right next door, has the same owner, the same chef and of course the same (very high) level of cuisine, albeit in a more low-key atmosphere.

 BILLILI
136, RUE DU FAUBOURG POISSONNIÈRE
75010 PARIS

Tue-Sat: midday / 3pm and 6:30pm / 10:30pm	No reservations	Metro: Poissonnière, Gare-du-Nord or Barbès-Rochechouart

BILLILI

© DAN ASSAYAG

BILLILI

© DAN ASSAYAG

LES ARLOTS
136, RUE DU FAUBOURG POISSONNIÈRE
75010 PARIS

| Tue–Sat:
midday / 2pm
and 7:30pm / 10pm | Reservation: +33 1 42 82 92 01 | Metro: Poissonnière, Gare-du-Nord
or Barbès-Rochechouart |

ONE OF THE CAPITAL'S
GREATEST ARCHITECTURAL SURPRISES

Located off the beaten tourist track, the Palais de la Porte-Dorée is nonetheless one of Paris's greatest architectural surprises.

In addition to the enormous bas-relief that adorns the facade, don't miss the central hall (known as the Forum), with its exceptional frescoes painted by Pierre-Henri Ducos de La Haille on the theme of the French colonies. The juxtaposition of these frescoes and the equally magnificent mosaic floor makes for a truly spectacular ensemble.

 PALAIS DE LA PORTE-DORÉE
293, AVENUE DAUMESNIL
75012 PARIS

Tue-Fri: 10am / 5:30pm Sat-Sun: 10am / 7pm Mon: closed	+ 33 1 53 59 58 60 Visit of the central hall and glimpse of the two oval salons: free	Metro: Porte Dorée

Built by French architect Albert Laprade for the Paris Colonial Exposition of 1931, the Palais de la Porte-Dorée also boasts two beautiful Art Deco oval salons on either side of the entrance hall. They once served as the offices of the colonial administrator, Hubert Lyautey.

ICE CREAM
DONE DIFFERENTLY

Founded in 1976, La Tropicale Glacier is a truly unique ice-cream parlour. This charming place on the corner of Rue de Prague and Rue Emilio Castelar, a ten-minute walk from Gare de Lyon, is definitely off the beaten track: mango and chilli flakes, turmeric and grapefruit, pumpkin and orange, cocoa and smoked whisky ... It's a far cry from strawberry or vanilla – even when the latter supposedly comes from Madagascar ...

The flavours change regularly according to the season. The ice creams are always made from the finest ingredients supplied by the best producers, with an emphasis on fair pay, fair trade and short supply chains.

What's more, you can expect a warm welcome.

 LA TROPICALE GLACIER
7, RUE DE PRAGUE
75012 PARIS

+33 1 42 16 87 27
latropicaleglacier.com
Metro: Ledru-Rollin

 LA TROPICALE GLACIER
180, BVD VINCENT AURIOL
75013 PARIS

+33 9 83 81 41 29
latropicaleglacier.com
Metro: Place d'Italie

THE MOST BEAUTIFUL RESTAURANT
IN THE WORLD?

Built for the 1900 Paris Exposition, Le Train Bleu is arguably the most beautiful restaurant in Paris, if not the world.

Decorated with paintings showing the various destinations of the trains departing from the Gare de Lyon, it is housed within the station itself, on the first floor in front of the main platforms.

Oddly enough, many Parisians – never mind tourists – don't know about it. And yet it exerts such fascination that some regulars even make the round-trip journey by train from Dijon or Lyon in a single day just to go there for lunch …

The classic French cuisine is decent, though priced too high for the quality on offer, but that's not why you come …

Bask in the atmosphere and admire the decor and you'll have an excellent time, making it well worth arriving early if you have an afternoon or evening train to catch.

 LE TRAIN BLEU
1ST FLOOR, GARE DE LYON
PLACE LOUIS ARMAND, HALL 1
75012 PARIS

+ 33 1 43 43 09 06 le-train-bleu.com	Reservations are essential	Metro and RER: Gare de Lyon

For those who love the atmosphere of chic brasseries, Le Grand Colbert, near the Palais-Royal, is another magnificent restaurant (without the paintings from 1900) which offers superior quality food at more reasonable prices.

LE GRAND COLBERT
2, RUE VIVIENNE
75002 PARIS

+33 1 42 86 87 88
legrandcolbert.fr

Metro: Bourse

THE GO-TO
RESTAURANT
OF MANY PARISIAN
FOODIES

For many Parisian foodies, Café Les Deux Gares is their favourite restaurant. And it really does have it all: friendly service, quality products and cuisine, reasonable prices, a lovely sunny terrace away from street noise, and a brilliantly executed neo-bistro interior with retro charm...

You're sure to have a lovely time here, just above the Gare de l'Est and a stone's throw from the Gare du Nord (hence the name). It's the perfect place to go before catching your train to Strasbourg, Lille, Brussels, or London.

 CAFÉ LES DEUX GARES
1, RUE DES DEUX GARES
75010 PARIS

| MON–FRI: 9am / midnight
SAT: 10am / midnight
SUN: closed | +33 1 40 38 17 05
hoteldeuxgares.com/fr/cafe.html | Metro: Gare de l'Est |

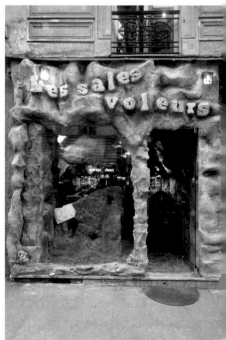

THE COOLEST
THRIFT STORE
IN PARIS

Pénitencier des Sales Voleurs (Dirty Thieves' Penitentiary): the storefront sets the tone ...

Whether in the 20th, 15th or 5th arrondissement, Les Sales Voleurs are thrift stores with a pretty crazy decor (prison, bank or cave, depending on the location) where you can find clothes at prices that change every day.

The entire stock is replaced on Fridays and Sundays, so those are the days when the prices are highest – but also when you get the most choice.

For some really great bargains, go on a Thursday, when everything is just €0.95.

FRIPERIES LES SALES VOLEURS 285, RUE DE VAUGIRARD 75015 PARIS	42, RUE MONGE 75005 PARIS	31, RUE D'AVRON 75020 PARIS
Daily: 10am / 7pm Metro: Vaugirard	Daily: 10am / 7pm Metro: Cardinal Lemoine	Daily: 10am / 7pm Metro: Buzenval

A COSY BAR
WITH BRITISH CHARM

The library-bar in the magnificent Hôtel Saint-James is a charming and elegant little gem that even many Parisians haven't been to, thinking that it's a private club. Yet the bar is open to the public in the evenings from 7pm.

Wooden floors, antique carpets, comfortable leather and velvet armchairs, a coffered ceiling, bookcases with a spiral staircase on one side and large windows overlooking the garden on the other – the decor of this bar, with its typically British, hushed ambience, verges on perfection.

The intimate atmosphere is perfect for a romantic rendezvous. And if everything goes according to plan, you can always book a room in the hotel to finish off the evening ...

It's also the ideal place to sit and read quietly. In summer, you can enjoy a drink in the charming garden, accompanied by a short à la carte menu.

 LIBRARY-BAR OF THE HÔTEL SAINT-JAMES
5, PLACE DU CHANCELIER ADENAUER
75116 PARIS

Daily: 8:30am / midnight for hotel members and guests Daily: 7pm / midnight for the general public	+33 1 44 05 81 81 contact@saint-james-paris.com	Metro: Porte Dauphine

EXPERIENCE
THE SACRED SOUL
OF PARIS

France is the eldest daughter of the Catholic Church and Paris is its capital (to find out why, see our other guide to the city, *Secret Paris*).

One of the most spiritual ways to experience the city's sacred soul is by taking part in the perpetual adoration at Sacré-Cœur in Montmartre: since 1 August 1885, people have been praying in the basilica non-stop, day and night, seven days a week – including during two world wars and the Covid pandemic.

And anyone can participate. Just book your spot – by phone, online or even on site (sometimes for the same day) – and choose an option: dormitory, single or shared room (all very reasonably priced). On the day of your reservation, go to the reception before 9:30pm and sign up for at least one hour-long slot between 11pm and 7am.

**PERPETUAL ADORATION
AT SACRÉ-CŒUR BASILICA
35, RUE DU CHEVALIER DE LA BARRE
75018 PARIS**

+33 1 53 41 89 00

sacre-coeur-montmartre.com/
hotellerie-et-groupes/
lhotellerie-de-la-basilique/
participer-a-une-nuit-dadoration

Metro: Abbesses

At 10pm there is a public mass. At 11pm, when the basilica closes, only those who have signed up for the perpetual adoration stay on. It is now time for the night of prayer before the Blessed Sacrament to begin, in an atmosphere of faith, fervour and true reverence. You can stay longer than planned, rest in your room if you're tired, come back again later or wander alone in the half-lit basilica (in silence, of course).

It's a truly magical experience for Catholics, but not only: no questions are asked at the reception. Catholics, Christians and adherents of other faiths are all welcome to come together for part of the night for this extraordinary shared experience.

When you leave the basilica in the early morning, you'll be filled with a strange sense of wellbeing.

 # 29

HAVE MONTMARTRE
ALL TO YOURSELF

Montmartre is probably our favourite district in Paris – unfortunately, it's overrun with people almost all year round. That's why we recommend this short alternative route: it will allow you to steer clear of the crowds at Place du Tertre (which should be avoided at all costs) and the Sacré-Coeur while taking you to the most authentic part of the district, still frequented by locals.

Get off the metro at Lamarck-Caulaincourt, go up the stairs and walk along Avenue Junot, one of the most beautiful in Paris. Maison Tristan Tzara (designed by Adolf Loos and built in 1926) is at No. 15. Villa Léandre (No. 23 ter) is a dead-end street with pretty, low brick houses in the Anglo-Norman style, overgrown with climbing plants. At the far end of the avenue, note the doorway to No. 4, which looks like the blades of a windmill (there used to be several windmills in the area).

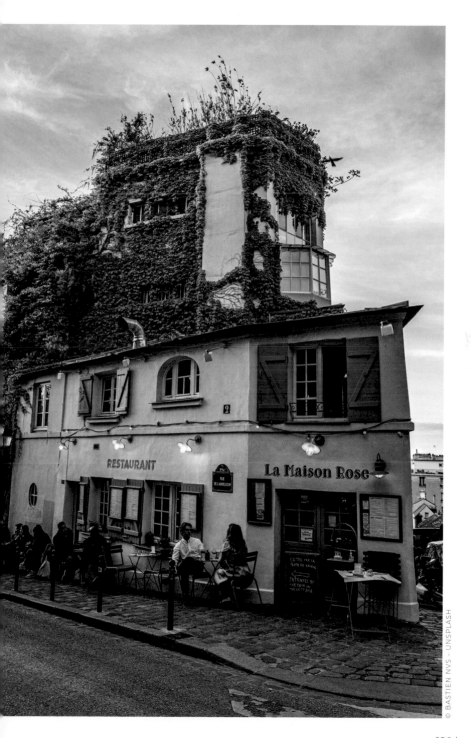

At 21 Avenue Junot, Passage Lepic-Junot, in the heart of the former maquis of Montmartre, is now closed off by a gate. You have two options: either ring the intercom of the pétanque court to play a game followed by a drink at the bar, or go into the Hôtel Particulier (see page 134) for a bite to eat or a drink (starting from breakfast).

Retrace your steps to 1 Avenue Junot, one of the most beautiful private residences in all of Paris. If by some miracle the door happens to open in front of you, politely ask the resident(s) if you can peek inside this fantastic spot where vines grow and rabbits frolic at the foot of the Moulin Blute-Fin.

You'll soon spot the Moulin Blute-Fin on the left, one of the last two mills in Paris along with the Moulin Radet (better known as the Moulin de la Galette), though the latter is no longer at its original location.

Walking back up the avenue on the left, make a detour to 11 Avenue Junot to see the Hameau des Artistes (Artists' Hamlet) from the outside, which links Avenue Junot to Rue Lepic (at No. 75) and is usually locked, requiring an access code to enter.

Retrace your steps to the beginning of Avenue Junot and Place Marcel Aymé, where you can spot the amusing *Le Passe-Muraille* ('The Man Who Walked through Walls'), a sculptural tribute to Aymé's novel of the same name.

As you go down Rue de l'Abreuvoir, you'll see on the right a number of houses and artists' studios nestled in a large natural park. A sort of Parisian Villa Medici, this site rents modestly priced studios (ranging from 60 to 100 square metres) to foreign artists for a year. Just below, Place Dalida has superb views of the Sacré-Coeur – probably the most panoramic views in the entire city.

In the square stands a bronze bust of the singer Dalida. You can caress her ample bosom to give it a patina to rival that of Juliet's breasts in Verona (and maybe for a bit of good luck, if you're superstitious). Then head right, up towards the vineyards. The metro is just a short walk away.

NB: The doors of 45 Rue Lepic open unexpectedly onto an alley lined with artists' and artisans' studios.

© GUILLAUME GRASSET

On the hill, at the heart of this itinerary, is a little-known café that is the perfect place for a break away from the crowds. Les 5 Marches serves simple, delicious dishes for lunch in a pretty setting.

 LES 5 MARCHES
12, RUE GIRARDON
75018 PARIS

Mon and Tue: 10am / 3pm	5marches-montmartre.com	Metro: Lamarck-Caulaincourt
Wed–Fri: 10am / 5pm		
Sat and Sun: 10am / 6pm		

A LUXURY HOTEL,
LIKE OUT IN THE COUNTRY

Tucked away in the heart of the most beautiful part of Montmartre, the Hôtel Particulier is a true gem: exquisitely tasteful, luxurious, comfortable rooms, and a garden where you can have breakfast (or more) when the weather is nice, all in a charming, romantic setting.

The hotel has just five suites, each in a different style and all magnificent!

If you can't afford to spend a night here, take advantage of the restaurant (which is open to the public) to gain access to this special place in what is one of if not the most charming areas of the city.

Go on, treat yourself!

 L'HÔTEL PARTICULIER
23, AVENUE JUNOT, PAVILLON D
75018 PARIS

+33 1 53 41 81 40 | hotelparticulier.com | Metro: Lamarck-Caulaincourt

THANKS

Florence Amiel, Dan Assayag, Mathilde Bargibant, Émilie de Beaumont, Kees & Aude van Beek, Emmanuel Bérard, Florent Billioud, Antoine Blachez, Philippe Bonfils, Ghislaine Bouchet, Jean-Claude Boulliard, Pierrick Bourgault, Louis-Marie Bourgeois, Jean-Baptiste Bourgeois, Marie & Brandino Brandolini, Jean-Laurent Cassely, Philippe Darmayan, Stéphane & Géraldine Decaux, Simon Edelstein, Vincent Formery, Servane & Giovanni Giol, Philippe Gloaguen, Amaël Gohier, Azmina Goulamaly, Alexandre Guérin, Ines Guérin, Patrick Haas, Elvire Haberman, Catherine Ivanichtchenko, Antoine Jonglez, Aurélie Jonglez, Louis Jonglez, Romaine Jonglez, Stéphanie & Guillaume Jonglez, Timothée & Delphine Jonglez, Benoît de Larouzière, Xavier & Sophie Lièvre, Clémence Mathé, Olivier & Valérie de Panafieu, Marianne & Fabrice Perreau-Saussine, Hélène Poulit, Alireza Razavi, Valérie Renaud, Stéphanie Rivoal, Dominique Roger, Béatrice & Pierre Rosenberg, Bertrand Saint Guilhem, Hervé Schlosser, Damien Seyrieix, François Simon, Ambroise Tézenas, Victoire & Olivier de Trogoff, Marie-Christine Valla, Delphine Valluet, Henri & Natacha Villeroy, Ézechiel Zerah.

Special thanks to Fany Péchiodat for the concept behind the collection.

This book was created by:

Thomas Jonglez, author

Emmanuelle Willard Toulemonde, layout

Sophie Schlondorff, translator

Janah Gough, editing

Kimberly Bess, proofreading

Roberto Sassi, publishing

You can write to us at contact@soul-of-cities.com

Follow us on Instagram on @jonglez_publishing

In the same collection:

Soul of Amsterdam
Soul of Athens
Soul of Barcelona
Soul of Berlin
Soul of Kyoto
Soul of Lisbon
Soul of Los Angeles
Soul of Marrakesh
Soul of New York
Soul of Rome
Soul of Tokyo
Soul of Venice

Cover: © Bastien Nvs – Unsplash
Back cover designed by Freepik

© JONGLEZ 2024
Registration of copyright: June 2024 – Edition: 01
ISBN: 978-2-36195-760-5
Printed in Slovakia by Polygraf